BRIGHTON
AND
HOVE
IN OLD PHOTOGRAPHS

BRIGHTON
AND
HOVE
IN OLD PHOTOGRAPHS

COLLECTED BY
JUDY MIDDLETON

ALAN SUTTON
1988

Alan Sutton Publishing Limited
Brunswick Road · Gloucester

First published 1988

British Library Cataloguing in Publication Data

Brighton and Hove in old photographs
1. East Sussex. Hove, history 2. East Sussex.
Brighton, history
I. Middleton, Judy
942.2'54

ISBN 0-86299-540-X

Typesetting and origination by
Alan Sutton Publishing Limited.
Printed in Great Britain
by WBC Print Limited.

CONTENTS

INTRODUCTION

Brighton – the very name conjures up a kaleidoscope of images – sea and sun, deckchairs and candyfloss, the Royal Pavilion and Regency terraces, the piers and the Downs. The list is endless. So it should come as no surprise that there is still scope for another book of old photographs.

The net has been cast wide to gather in as much variety as possible. There are photographs of Edwardian ladies promenading in their elegant dresses but there are also the working folk; the fishermen and the labourers. There are images of the Royal Pavilion but there are small shops with crowded windows too. There are amusements on the piers and ploughing on the Downs, overcrowded horse-buses and splendid early motor vehicles.

Richard Jeffries once praised the clear quality of the Brighton light, so it is fitting that in such a place India should have provided architectural inspiration – the domes, minarets and lattice work are as much a motif as the Brighton dolphin.

The original Indian dream dates back to the Prince Regent to whom Brighton owes its genesis as a fashionable watering place. He and the good Doctor Russell of course, who discovered the marvellous properties of sea water in treating various disorders and who published his celebrated work in 1761. Sea water was for drinking as well as for bathing in and Dr Russell heartily recommended his patients to come to Brighton. On the grounds that if a cure is nasty enough it is bound to be effective, taking the sea water became all the rage. As for the Prince, the sea air inspired him with dreams of Xanadu, as the poet puts it, and thus was born the Royal Pavilion; a unique amalgam of an Indian exterior and a Chinese interior.

As Brighton grew, so it absorbed into its boundaries separate communities which had once been villages in their own right. However, you can still find a village nucleus surviving here and there.

On the other hand there is Hove which, like a shy bride, as the newspaper chroniclers of the last century delighted to call her, has long resisted Brighton's attempt at a shot-gun wedding. Nevertheless, Hove owes her growth to the same social changes and her expansion began in the 1820s when fashionable society came to the smartest place in town – Brunswick Square and Terrace.

In the swings and roundabouts of fashion it is amusing to recall that Hove emerged from a small village well known for its smuggling proclivities, into a somewhat sedate Victorian town. Whereas neighbouring Portslade, for centuries esteemed as a favoured spot by important families, became hostess to a vigorous industrial life. Brighton's gas and electricity were produced here, while a tide of voluminous washing was sent to be dealt with in Portslade laundries.

This book is an attempt to capture some of the rich tapestry of life in the Brighton and Hove area. Some of the photographs date back to the nineteenth century, while others were taken as late as the 1940s or 1950s. But such is the accelerating pace of today's world that these pictures look every bit as nostalgic as the older ones.

Those associated with HMS *King Alfred* are of particular interest. Through the doors of this stone frigate (the erstwhile Hove Marina Swimming Baths) there streamed 22,500 men to be trained as RNVR officers during the Second World War. They were known as cadet ratings and wore a distinctive white cap band. When they had passed the final and dreaded Admiralty Board, they were known as OUTs (officers under training). Their contribution to the war effort was considerable. Many famous names are ex-*King Alfred* men; for instance Sir Peter Scott, Sir Alec Guiness, Kenneth More, Donald Sinden, Richard Baker, Norris McWhirter and Jon Pertwee.

It is perhaps superfluous to say that the sea has been important to Brighton – perhaps even its *raison d'être* if you like. However, in earlier times the sea was an element to be regarded with a certain amount of caution. The fishermen of the town wrested a precarious living from the sea by pushing the indigenous craft, called the hoggie, into the evening tide; but the sea could also bring raiders. The French were prone to descend in lightning raids and there was the memorable occasion when they razed the town by fire in 1514. A defensive wall was built in time to welcome the Spanish Armada which sailed up the Channel in 1588. Then there were the terrible storms and flooding. Portslade and Hove lost acres to the sea, and in the storms of 1703 and 1705 the sea obliterated 112 houses from the lower town of Brighton built below the cliffs. Brighton was so devastated by the latter that the town had to get out the begging bowl and seek help to build defensive groynes. At Hove too, the massive sea wall, so wonderfully constructed by our Victorian ancestors, at last put a stop to intermittent flooding.

In the second half of the eighteenth century, the sea suddenly became the bonus that Brighton needed. First it gained medicinal respect, then, as the sick of society flocked to Brighton, it became a place of fashion. Soon every other house took lodgers and brilliant new estates like Kemp Town and Brunswick Town were built fronting the sea. It was a novel idea to build houses looking out over the sea. The old town of Brighthelmston had tended to turn her back on it as far as possible, and even the Royal Pavilion had an east/west aspect.

The arrival of the railway in 1841 accelerated the growth. The railway also introduced a new species – the day tripper – who rolled off the trains in their thousands during the summer. Fashionable folk began to avoid Brighton during the tripper season and, by late Victorian times, the smart time to be at Brighton was in the winter season. It also gave the well-heeled a chance to avoid the suffocating London smogs.

As the network of roads and houses began to spread, parks and gardens were laid out and the town fathers took to extensive tree planting in the streets. The majority were elms because they were thought to withstand the salt spray better than other varieties. When Dutch elm disease was rampant in parts of Sussex in the 1970s, tree lovers in Brigthton and Hove held their breath. Although some were lost, close vigilance kept the toll to a minimum. Then came the October hurricane of 1987 and the carefully tended parks were devastated, while huge elms came crashing down in the Steine. Hove Park was one of the worst hit with barely 300 trees still standing out of a total of around 800. It is strange to recall how recent an amenity it is to enjoy having trees in Brighton. After all we need only to recall Dr Johnson's visit to Brighton in 1765 when he said the place was such a barren, treeless place that if you felt depressed you would be hard put to it to find a good branch from which to hang yourself.

Brighton continues to be a town of contrasts – the vulgar still jostles with the refined. Everybody finds something different to love or hate about the place, but dull it is not.

SECTION ONE

The Royal Pavilion

The Pavilion, Brighton.

THE GARDENS OF THE ROYAL PAVILION are being prepared for a party. Note the Chinese lanterns – no public occasion was considered complete without festoons of them in Victorian and Edwardian days.

THE CHARMING TWIN GATEWAYS at the south entrance to the Royal Pavilion in around 1910. They were removed after the First World War.

THE NEW SOUTH GATE being unveiled by the Maharaja of Patiala in October 1921. It was designed as a memorial to the Indian soldiers who were nursed at the Pavilion during the war. There were 28,000 volunteers from the Maharaja's state.

THIS WAS THE LIVELY SCENE when the Comite du Commerce France paid an official visit in 1907.

THE EAST FRONT OF THE PAVILION after a snowfall on 29 December 1908.

SECTION TWO

The Beach and Sea Front

PADDLING AT BRIGHTON.

PADDLING AT LOW TIDE with enough clothes and hats to make sure nobody suffered from sunburn.

A FAMILY GROUP ON THE PEBBLES near the bottom of West Street.

BRIGHTON (LOW TIDE AT BLACK ROCK). CHILDREN'S CORNER

BLACK ROCK was a favourite place with children because of the many small rock pools. This view has changed out of all recognition since the Marina was built.

THE FLIMSY TENTS AND BATHING CHALETS make a contrast to the solid buildings behind – note the old Bedford Hotel on the right.

A VIEW OF BRIGHTON BEACH at its most crowded, captured by A.L. Henderson in September 1890. The woman with the apron is selling ice-cream.

IT IS DIFFICULT TO MAKE OUT WHAT ALL THE EXCITEMENT IS ABOUT, but a lady (evangelist?), with outstretched arm, can just be seen at the centre.

PERHAPS A.L. HENDERSON SAMPLED SOME OF THE SHELLFISH from the stalls after photographing them in 1890.

ONE OF HENDERSON'S BEST PHOTOGRAPHS reproduced (like the previous four) from a glass negative. It was taken in September 1890 and shows the Hotel Metropole and the West Pier.

THE BEACH AT WESTERN HOVE in around 1912. Note the billowing changing tents which had to be taken down not later than an hour after sunset.

BATHERS ON HOVE BEACH in c. 1926.

A FINE VIEW OF THE ORIGINAL ENTRANCE TO THE AQUARIUM in c. 1908.

A FAMILY POSE ON THE BALUSTRADE of the steps leading down to the Aquarium in the 1920s. The notice states 'The Specimens are fed at 12 and 3'.

AN INTERESTING VIEW OF MADEIRA DRIVE because it shows that Volk's original railway track was mounted on wooden stilts.

THE PALACE PIER glimpsed through the cool arcades of the Madeira Walk.

A VIEW OF MARINE PARADE, with a gentleman riding a tricycle in front of the Royal Crescent Hotel on the left.

ANOTHER OF HENDERSON'S SPLENDID VIEWS with the Royal Albion Hotel in the background.

A CLEAR DAY in c. 1896. The Chain Pier is still intact and the Palace Pier is being built. Markwell's Hotel (now the Queen's) is on the left.

THIS PART OF KING'S ROAD HAS CHANGED CONSIDERABLY. The Old Ship Hotel is still there but the buildings behind the umbrellas have been replaced by the Ramada Renaissance Hotel.

LOOKING WESTWARD ALONG KING'S ROAD in 1890, near the bottom of West Street.

ALMOST AN ADVERTISEMENT for the decorative qualities of Victorian ironwork – note the shelter, railings and lampposts.

THE RESIDENTS OF REGENCY SQUARE complained bitterly when the West Pier was built opposite their quiet retreat in 1866.

THE GRAND HOTEL was designed by J.H. Whichcord and opened in 1864.

THIS STRETCH OF PROMENADE is dominated by the Hotel Metropole, opened in 1890 and designed by the great Victorian architect Alfred Waterhouse.

A NOSTALGIC PHOTOGRAPH of long dresses and the late lamented old Bedford Hotel, built in 1829 and destroyed by fire in April 1964.

THE END OF THE DAY — a middle-aged couple reflect.

THE BOATING POOL, next door to the West Pier, photographed in the 1920s.

The Promenade Brighton and Norfolk Hotel.

ANOTHER OF BRIGHTON'S ASSERTIVE VICTORIAN HOTELS; the Norfolk was built a year after the Grand.

A VIEW OF BRIGHTON which can be dated to 1893 because of the two lamp standards without any lamps. The sea-front electric lighting scheme was inaugurated on 16 September 1893.

SECTION THREE

Piers

LOOKING NORTH FROM THE END OF THE CHAIN PIER in c. 1870. When it was built in 1823 the Chain Pier was one of the engineering marvels of the age. The cast-iron towers weighed 15 tons each and every link in the suspension chain weighed 112lbs. It was designed by Captain Samuel Brown.

ANOTHER VIEW OF THE CHAIN PIER which reveals the massive timber piles on which it stood.

THIS WAS THE SAD SCENE AFTER THE STORM of 4/5 December 1896 when the Chain Pier was destroyed.

A NOSTALGIC GLIMPSE OF THE WEST PIER in the 1920s, when it was in a fine state of repair. It was designed by Eusebius Birch and opened on 6 October 1866.

A SUNNY DAY ON THE WEST PIER in the 1890s. Every lady carried an umbrella to protect her complexion – even the one in the rowing boat.

PROFESSOR REDDISH DIVING OFF THE WEST PIER in September 1890. He also gave swimming demonstrations in Brill's Baths.

BRIGHTON. — Prof. Doughtys Performing Dogs, West Pier. — LL.

PROFESSOR DOUGHTY AND HIS PERFORMING DOGS were another West Pier attraction. The dog in the centre might not be as docile as he looks for he wears a muzzle.

A REMARKABLY CLEAR VIEW of the sea front from the West Pier.

THE PALACE PIER in c. 1904 showing the ornate iron arches, of which there were 6 separate groups. The Palace Pier was opened on 20 May 1899.

THE PALACE PIER aglow with lights in the 1920s.

THE PALACE PIER FOLLIES were a hard-working group. In 1917 they went through their routine 3 times daily and twice on Sundays.

Beach and Front, Brighton, from Palace Pier.

THE PROSPECT FROM THE PALACE PIER in c. 1910. Note the row of bathing machines.

Boats and Fishing

A GROUP OF FISHERMEN on the beach in 1871. Note the clay pipes.

BRIGHTON BEACH in c. 1886. The huge capstans were necessary to haul the boats up the beach.

A MOMENT OF PEACE at the Fish Market.

75 BRIGHTON. — The Fish Market — LL

A SCENE AT THE FISH MARKET which epitomises the working side of Brighton beach.

76 BRIGHTON. — The Fish Market.

THE ACTIVITY AT THE FISH MARKET attracted as many spectators as customers.

THIS VIEW gives a clear indication of how fishing boats and bathing machines had to jostle for space.

PLENTY OF FISH JUMPING IN THE NET as the fishing lads help to pull it in. The thin boy on the right makes a vivid contrast with the well-dressed young girl nearby.

THE ROPE HOUSES on the beach in c. 1880. Note the nets spread out to dry on the old oak fencing which was replaced by cast-iron railings in 1886.

RICHARD GUNN beside the lifeboat *Sunlight No. 2* (financed by a well-known soap company), which was on station at Brighton from 1888 until 1904.

THE POPULAR PADDLE STEAMER *Brighton Queen*, built in 1897. After being taken over by the Admiralty during the First World War, she was sunk in 1915.

A FINE SHOT OF THE *Skylark* with sails set in c. 1888. She was something of a Brighton institution ('Anymore for the Skylark?') and she was owned by Captain Collins.

CAPTAIN COLLINS AND THE ORIGINAL CREW OF THE SKYLARK. Captain Collins stands on the left wearing his standard dress of white jacket and black straw boater.

THE CREWS WHO TOOK PART IN THE RNVR WHALER RACE at Hove in c. 1910. They were the Foretop Crew of No. 2 Company Naval Volunteers and the Elephant Crew of the Naval Volunteers. Lieutenant Stuart was the judge.

SECTION FIVE

Shops

FREDERICK HILLS, butcher (English Meat Only) at 57a Richmond Street, Brighton, in c. 1925.

WILLIAM GEORGE GROVES and his assistant, Charles Thatcher, outside his butcher's shop at 42 Gardner Street, Brighton, in the 1920s.

BALCHIN BROS., 62, QUEEN'S ROAD, BRIGHTON

WATCHMAKERS, JEWELLERS, AND FANCY STORES

THE BALCHIN BROTHERS' GLITTERING WINDOW DISPLAY at 62 Queen's Road was obviously designed to catch the eye of day trippers walking from the railway station.

THE CHEMIST'S SHOP at 144 Church Road, Hove, was owned from 1887 until 1898 by James Williamson, an early pioneer of moving films.

GLAISYER AND KEMP'S CHEMIST SHOP was established at 11 and 12 North Street, Brighton, in 1798 and stayed there until the lease ran out in 1924. The business transferred to Castle Square while Hanningtons took over the old premises. Both Glaisyer and Kemp came from Quaker families.

COWLEY'S OLD BUNN SHOPPE in Pool Valley was built in 1794 and faced with black mathematical tiles.

A VENERABLE PHOTOGRAPH taken in 1862 and showing W.J. Smith's bookshop in North Street.

THE PREMISES OF F.W. WITHERDEN AND SON of 18 Nile Street, photographed in 1870. They were ironmongers and gas fitters and locksmiths too.

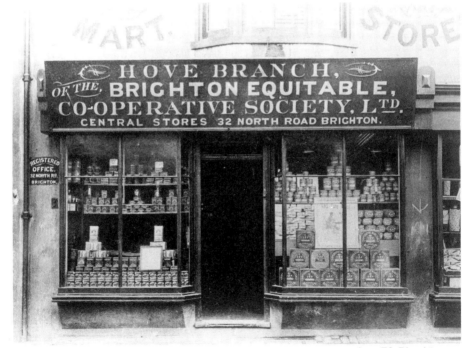

THE HOVE BRANCH OF THE BRIGHTON CO-OPERATIVE SOCIETY was opened at 78 Blatchington Road in 1920.

JAMES LEE'S GROCERY SHOP at 39 George Street in the 1920s.

THE SMALL REFRESHMENT HOUSE AT FALMER sold cups of tea as well as postcards.

SECTION SIX

Streets

A TRANQUIL VIEW OF THE HIGH STREET, Portslade Old Village, in c. 1908. The Grange on the left has gone, the Swiss Cottages in the background were demolished in the 1960s and the George Inn has been rebuilt.

SOUTHERN CROSS, PORTSLADE, in *c.* 1910. The pub on the left was demolished in the 1970s as part of the road-widening scheme.

A GROUP OF CHILDREN IN NORTH LANE, Portslade (now North Road) in *c.* 1910.

CHURCH ROAD, HOVE, in c. 1899 with a grand obstruction in the shape of the Brighton Brewery. It was demolished in c. 1904.

GEORGE STREET, HOVE, in 1914. Note the poles and wires for the experimental trolleybus, the Fire Station on the left and the advertising sweep's brush on the right.

THE TRAVELLER'S JOY INN on Hove sea front was demolished in 1908. It was replaced by the St Aubyns Hotel which has recently been renamed the Kingsway.

QUEEN'S ROAD, Brighton, in 1936.

THE WIDENING OF Western Road, Brighton, in August 1934.

NORTH STREET, BRIGHTON, in c. 1910. Note the colonnade leading round into New Road on the left. It was removed in 1929.

This photograph of BRIGHTON'S FAMOUS LANES dates from the 1920s.

WEST STREET in c. 1905. Although some of the buildings have changed (and not for the better) St Paul's still dominates the scene.

The Fashionable Scene

THIS VIEW SHOWS THE TEMPORARY BANDSTAND erected on the Hove Lawns in front of Brunswick Terrace. Top military bands were engaged to provide the music during these Edwardian summers.

Hove Lawns and West Pier, Brighton

PLENTY OF SEATS were provided for those who wanted to watch the fashionable world go by.

Church Parade, Hove Lawns   Published by Pictorial Centre, 7 Grand Junction Road, Brighton   56112

PROMENADING ON THE HOVE LAWNS on a Sunday morning was a social event of importance.

A WELL-ATTENDED MUNICIPAL GARDEN PARTY held in June 1935 in the grounds of the Royal Pavilion.

ALDERMAN BRUCE MORISON was Mayor of Hove from 1905 to 1907. He is photographed here at his Patcham home 'Woodslee'.

ALDERMAN BRUCE MORISON gave a garden party on the Hove Lawns in June 1906. There were 2,000 guests and music from the band of the 20th Hussars.

HOVE HORSE TRIALS were held on 28 June 1908 at the Marine Park, now known as Wish Park.

HIS MAJESTY THE LATE KING IN HIS FAVOURITE SEAT AT HOVE.

KING EDWARD VII visited Hove in 1907, 1908 and 1910. He found the sea air good for his health.

SECTION EIGHT

A Working Life

THIS PHOTOGRAPH WAS TAKEN IN 1897 during the extension of the Medina Esplanade at Hove. The engineer was H.H. Scott. The cranes belong to J. Parsons and Sons, builders – a name still familiar today.

A BUILDING SITE AT FISHERSGATE in the 1920s. Note the wooden scaffolding poles. William George Ring stands on the extreme left.

THE DEMOLITION OF THE OLD AQUARIUM ENTRANCE in 1929. The statues represent the Four Seasons and, although rescued at the time, they have since disappeared.

AN OLD PHOTOGRAPH TAKEN IN 1858 which captures the demolition of the West Battery. The Grand Hotel was built on the site of the old Battery House, where the naval lieutenant in charge of the Battery was stationed.

THE OLD ESTABLISHED FIRM OF ENGINEERS, PALMER AND COMPANY, photographed in c. 1895. They supplied the gas fittings for the Royal Pavilion in 1821. The firm was at 146 North Street, Brighton, from 1845 until 1904.

THE REGENT FOUNDRY at 63 North Road in c. 1900. It was formerly Reed's Foundry and, from a small shed in the yard, electricity was first generated for private consumers in the 1880s.

THOMAS THORNS (1869–1942) photographed in the luxuriant conservatory of 27 Shaftesbury Road, Brighton, with his employer Mr Turner. Note the abundance of grapes and two parrot cages in the background.

A BLIND MUSICIAN photographed on the sea front in September 1890 by A.L. Henderson.

CHILD MINSTRELS performing in September 1890 outside the recently-opened Hotel Metropole.

HUGH BURGESS, blacksmith, standing on the right outside the Old Forge, Portslade, in c. 1900.

BILL PATCHING ploughing at North House Farm, Portslade, in c. 1930.

LAND GIRLS AT PORTSLADE in 1917. Amy Broomfield is the girl perched on the right while cousin Harry balances precariously on top.

PEA PICKERS at Smokey House Farm, Portslade, in c. 1900.

A NOSTALGIC STUDY OF A SHEPHERD WITH HIS FLOCK near Falmer, at a time when the South Downs were still well-stocked with sheep.

HARVESTING in the time-honoured way at Falmer.

A GROUP OF JOCKEYS at Mile Oak Paddocks in around 1914. One of their horses won the Derby in 1910. Molly Archer was their housekeeper and she lived with her family in the waterworks cottage nearby. The jockey on her left is Tommy Avery.

THE HOVE FIRE BRIGADE outside their George Street Fire Station which was in operation from 1879 until 1926.

THE PORTSLADE FIRE BRIGADE pictured in August 1912. Standing at the far left is Jack Hustings and his brother-in-law, George Peirce, is third from the left. The Chief Fire Officer is Albert Walter Hillman.

THE STAFF OF THE FILLING DEPARTMENT AT RONUK'S, Portslade, in c. 1916. The factory produced a well-known floor polish. Back row from left to right: George Skinner, Bert Short, Jack Smith, Fred Peirce, Fred Parsons, Arthur Packham, Fred Twine, Reg Scutt and Cyril Brenchley. Second row: Chris Holland, Elsie Saunders, Emmie Packham, Mr Knight (foreman), Ivy Priestly and Archie Paris. Front row: Ernie Trussler, Frank Bernard and Vic Terry. Later Elsie married Fred Peirce and Emmie married Cyril Brenchley.

THE BRITANNIA FLOUR MILLS at Portslade pictured in c. 1914. In the background the spire of the Catholic church (opened in 1912) is visible.

Canal Portslade, Showing Electric Light Works.

THE ELECTRICITY WORKS at Portslade in c. 1906. Note the little boat which was used to ferry workers to the site.

THE NORTH WALL OF THE DOCK AT SOUTHWICK collapsed on 16 April 1907, virtually shutting off the canal and marooning the gas and electric works at Portslade.

PEGGY DUDENEY working at Tate's Laundry in c. 1909.

SECTION NINE

Transport

THE MOTOR CAR 'PRESENT TIMES' outside the Hotel Metropole in 1896.

THIS HORSE-BUS, photographed in c. 1901, ran from Hove to Castle Square. The driver is Fred Maslen and the conductor is Charles Miller.

A SPLENDID VIEW OF CHURCH ROAD, Hove, in c. 1904, complete with crowded horse-buses.

THE MEMBERS OF THE CLIFTONVILLE HOTEL CLUB BEANFEAST are all set for their outing from Hove in 1913.

THE LAST HORSE–DRAWN CARRIER, Shergold, leaving Brighton Place in February 1926.

THE ROYAL PARCEL MAIL outside the Ship Street Post Office in 1905.

A HORSE-DRAWN TRAM outside Brooker Hall, New Church Road, Hove, in c. 1900.

A WAGONETTE taking sightseers from West Street, Brighton, to Devil's Dyke in 1895.

A MOTOR BUS outside the Royal Oak, Rottingdean. Note the ladies descending from the top deck.

GRANDMA MARSH photographed in Hove Street in c. 1908, sitting in her Bath chair with her two dogs for company.

BRIGHTON'S FIRST MOTOR RACE WEEK was held in July 1905 on the new tarmac surface of Madeira Drive.

THE DRIVER S.F. EDGE is pictured here at the wheel of the 90hp Napier in which he won the Autocar Challenge Cup, travelling at 97.20 miles per hour.

SPECTATORS WATCH A TRAM struggling through the snow in December 1908.

TRAMS IN CHURCH STREET, Brighton, in c. 1905.

THE CEDES GEARLESS TRACKLESS TROLLEY-BUS made an experimental run down Goldstone Villas and George Street, Hove, in September 1914.

Corporation Tramways.   Brighton.

THE TRAM TERMINUS was located at the Old Steine from 1904 until 1939 when trams stopped running.

THE 'VENTURE' with its magnificent matched horses outside the Hotel Metropole in 1909. The coach was financed by the young American millionaire Alfred D. Vanderbilt.

WARTIME HOUSE REFUSE COLLECTION in Ditchling Road c. 1918. In the centre is the driver, William Thomas Harrop-Roller.

THE FIRST BATCH OF WAR-WOUNDED REACHED BRIGHTON, in September 1914 and were taken by motor ambulance to the Second Eastern General Hospital – the commandeered Brighton, Hove and Sussex Grammar School.

AN AMBULANCE drawn up at the entrance to the Indian Military Hospital c. 1916.

THE DYKE RAILWAY was in operation from 1887 until 1938.

-/- Steep Grade Railway, *to explain below, to of, at the* Devil's Dyke,

THE DYKE STEEP GRADE RAILWAY was opened in 1897 and lasted until 1908.

A HIGHLY-POLISHED FIRE ENGINE at Brighton Station. The monogram of the London, Brighton and South Coast Railway can be seen clearly.

A CHARABANC EXCURSION photographed in the 1920s at Madeira Drive.

MEMBERS OF THE CLARENDON CLUB outside their meeting place at 50 Clarendon Villas, Hove, in 1922.

THIS VAN, BELONGING TO C. AYRES, coal merchant, was photographed outside his premises at 1 Beaconsfield Road, Portslade, c. 1934.

MOTOR BUSES CD 103 and CD 236 outside the Connaught Hotel in Hove Street in 1904. From left to right: Arthur Dunn (driver), Charlie Cobden (conductor), Jack Ellis (driver), Fred Maslen (driver), George Tongue (conductor) and Charlie Miller (driver).

CHANTRAY'S STATUE OF GEORGE IV (weighing 30 tons) being removed in March 1922 to make way for the war memorial.

A TANKER EMERGING ONTO THE QUIET COASTAL ROAD in the 1920s, with one of the famous Mystery Towers at Southwick in the background.

MAGNUS VOLK (1851–1937) in his electric dogcart c. 1920. With him is his sister-in-law Deborah and his son Bert.

VOLK'S ELECTRIC RAILWAY was opened in 1883 and it is still going strong today, although it no longer runs over this particular stretch of track.

MAGNUS VOLK also created the Rottingdean Seashore Electric Railway which ran from 1896 until 1901. It was nicknamed 'Daddy Longlegs'.

THE SALOON OF THE DADDY LONGLEGS was 12 feet wide and 25 feet long and comfortably furnished.

GOAT CARTS, HORSE CABS AND A CHARMING FLOWER SELLER await customers on the Hove sea front in the 1890s.

A GOAT CART ON MADEIRA DRIVE with a little girl whose wide smile appears on other Brighton postcards.

THE BEACH WAS TOO PEBBLY FOR DONKEY RIDES so the obvious answer was the lower esplanade.

A MEETING OF CYCLISTS at the Old Steine in 1877.

THREE LADY CYCLISTS in Cowper Street, Hove, in 1905.

A MOTOR RALLY outside the Old Ship Hotel in 1908. In 1906 the Old Ship had become the headquarters of the Automobile Club.

Sports and Pastimes

AN ORDERLY, WELL-HATTED CROWD at the Albion v. Huddersfield match in 1922. There were 22,241 spectators.

J.CLAYTON. R.WHITING. W.TUSTIN. J.R.ROBSON.
R.HULME. A.LLOYD. J.LEEMING. T.STEWART. T.MORRIS. J.WILSON. J.ATKINSON. T.TURNER.
J.HALL. F.CRUMP. T.W.GRIERSON. A.E.LONGSTAFFE. J.MARTIN. J.ROBERTSON. J.JEE. R.ISHERWOOD.
J.BRENNAN. W.BOOTH

THE BRIGHTON AND HOVE ALBION TEAM for the 1908–1909 season. This was the team which beat Division 1 champions Aston Villa.

BRIGHTON AND HOVE ALBION FOOTBALL CLUB STAFF in 1925. Behind the man with the bowler hat and the walrus moustache stands the trainer, Mr Nealms, wearing a knitted waistcoat.

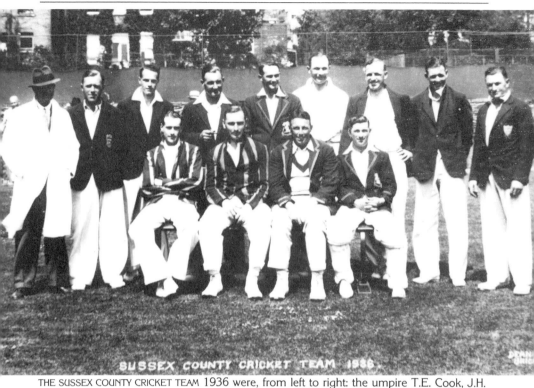

THE SUSSEX COUNTY CRICKET TEAM 1936 were, from left to right: the umpire T.E. Cook, J.H. Cornford, A.F. Wensley, James Langridge, John Langridge, H.W. Parks, C. Oakes, J.H. Parks. Front row: A. Melville, A.J. Holmes (Captain), M.W. Tate and W.L. Cornford.

THESE FISHERMEN are taking part in an Angler's Festival on the Palace Pier in November 1934.

A PUNCH AND JUDY SHOW in progress on Hove sea front on 17 August 1935.

LOOKING AT THIS HAPPY GROUP OF GIRLS it is hard to realize that the Second World War was declared only days later. Betram Mills's Circus visited Brighton in August 1939.

'LORD' GEORGE SANGER of circus fame photographed in c. 1897 in a large field between New Church Road and Portland Road, Hove.

BRIGHTON AND HOVE BOYS BRIGADE in camp at Sompting in 1910.

A ONE-MAN BAND and an inquisitive small boy are captured in this evocative photograph taken at Brighton in September 1950.

A SCENE INSIDE THE OLD HOVE BATHS C. 1914. The notice says 'Warning Don't Run'.

'OUR HOVE ALLOTMENT AT LANGDALE ROAD' with Willie, Mary and Frank.

DON THOMPSON (known as the Mighty Mouse) winning the London to Brighton walk in September 1960.

TWO BRIGHTON TIGERS, part of a famous ice-hockey team, photographed after beating Altrincham Aces 22–4 in June 1964.

Education and Health

DRILL CLASS in c. 1900 was not a popular event judging from the expression on their faces.

A CLASS OF TOUGH-LOOKING BOYS at St Nicolas's School, Portslade c. 1922. Their teacher, Miss Austin (later Mrs Gates), stands at the back.

STAFF AT THE ELLEN STREET SCHOOL, Hove, C. 1900. Alice Botton, pupil teacher, stands in the middle of the back row.

A PARTY FROM HABERDASHERS' ASKE'S SCHOOL visit the Sussex Room at Hove Museum in October 1939.

WINDLESHAM HOUSE SCHOOL, Portslade, stood in a 27-acre estate stretching from the High Street to the Old Shoreham Road. The fields have long since been submerged under housing.

TWO YOUNG READERS choose books at Hove Children's Library in 1953. Note the plain bindings of the books.

THE CHILDREN'S HOSPITAL in Dyke Road in 1903, before the balconies were erected.

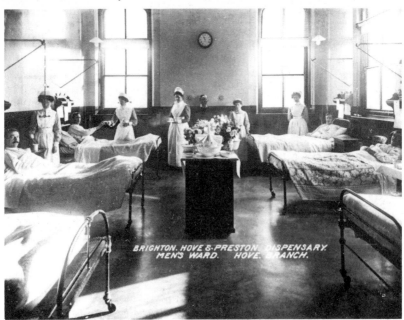

THE MEN'S WARD AT HOVE HOSPITAL in around 1912. The hospital celebrated its centenary in 1988.

SECTION TWELVE

Celebrations

A HUGE CROWD turns out to watch this procession along Madeira Drive at the turn of the century.

THE SAILORS seem to attract more small boys than anyone else.

A PROCESSION OF CHILDREN walking up the Drive to celebrate the opening of Hove Park on 24 May 1906.

TO CELEBRATE THE SILVER JUBILEE in May 1935 the Mayor of Hove (Councillor C.S. Loadsman), the Mayoress and the councillors in new robes walk to an open-air service on the Lawns.

BRIGHTON CELEBRATED THE SILVER JUBILEE OF KING GEORGE V AND QUEEN MARY in its own fashion. This was how East Street looked in May 1935.

A STREET PARTY IN LOWER PORTSLADE in full swing on 12 May 1937, to honour the coronation of King George VI and Queen Elizabeth. Printed from a glass negative.

AUGUST 1945 and the crowds are out to celebrate VJ Day. The soldier on the left with bent knee has obviously seen all Shirley Temple's films because he is aping her famous pose. The photograph was taken in East Street and English's Oyster Bar can be seen on the left.

SECTION THIRTEEN

People

A GROUP OF PEOPLE gathered together for a funeral. On the left is 18-year-old Emma Packham who lived at 73 Wolseley Road, Portslade, married a sailor and had seven children.

MRS SARAH GRIGSON outside 49 Abinger Road, Portslade, c. 1919, where she and her blacksmith husband brought up 13 children.

THE PETERS FAMILY at the back of 29 Elm Road, Portslade, in 1918. Fred Peters ran a market garden and the last miller in Portslade was a member of the family.

A HAPPY WEDDING GROUP outside Cowhayes Farm, Portslade, in 1919. The bridegroom is Albert Goacher and the bride is Miss Harwood (her father stands on the extreme left). The small boy wearing a sailor hat is Cecil Peters.

WILLIAM GROVES (BUTCHER) AND EDITH THORNS (who became a children's maid at 14 years of age) on their wedding day at Brighton on 7 April 1924. The bride wears a dress of crêpe de chine and carries a veritable garden of carnations and stocks.

MRS ELIZABETH HUSTINGS about to descend into the air-raid shelter in the garden of her house in Bampfield Street, Portslade, during the Second World War.

THE CHOIR OF ST NICOLAS'S CHURCH, Portslade, c. 1924. Back row from the left: Hector Coustick, ? Grundy, Albert Perry, Alfred Perry, Horace Chandler, Perce Cranham, Jack Rook and Ben Baldock. Second row: Alwyn Hyde, Mr Perry (father of Albert and Alfred), Mr White (organist), Revd Donald Campbell (vicar), Archie Greenyer, Horace Hore, –?–. Front row: Jim Noakes, Harry Clarke, Charles Hickling, George Hammond, Hector Hudson, John Rook (son of Jack).

N.J. BOOTH, Special Constable number 16, photo-graphed c. 1914.

HERR FRANZ MEISEL, Musical Director of Brighton Corporation Band which was based at the Aquar-ium and lasted from 1908 until 1918.

Parks and Gardens

A SPLENDID VIEW OF THE VICTORIA FOUNTAIN in the 1920s. It was erected to honour the young Queen Victoria in 1846, and was designed by A.H. Wilds.

THE WAY THEY USED TO MOW THE GRASS and roll the croquet pitch in Preston Park. The horses wore bootees to prevent their hooves cutting up the turf.

VICTORIA GARDENS was (and still is) an oasis of green in a busy thoroughfare. Note the tram on the left.

A SUMMER'S DAY in Queen's Park c. 1904.

THIS PHOTOGRAPH, TAKEN IN QUEEN'S PARK, turned out to be a very popular postcard and several versions were published.

SNOW SCENES AT HOVE · FEB · 1912. — ENTRANCE TO STANN'S WELL

WILES HOVE (1)

A SNOW SCENE at St Ann's Well Gardens, Hove, on 4 February 1912.

Brighton   St. Ann's Well

THE PUMP HOUSE in St Ann's Well pictured c. 1903. At one time the fashionable throng came here to drink the waters of the chalybeate spring.

PLAYING BOWLS at St Ann's Well in the 1920s.

HOVE PARK was opened on 24 May 1906. The Mayor, Alderman Bruce Morison, is about to unlock the gates.

A TRANQUIL SCENE IN EASTHILL PARK, Portslade, in the 1950s. The war memorial is clearly visible.

SECTION FIFTEEN

Military Matters

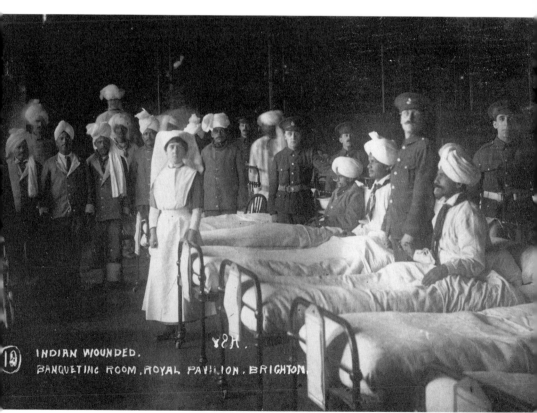

INDIAN WOUNDED.
BANQUETING ROOM, ROYAL PAVILION, BRIGHTON

THE MAGNIFICENT BANQUETING ROOM of the Royal Pavilion became one of the wards of the
Indian Military Hospital during the First World War.

A PARTY OF INDIAN CONVALESCENTS from the Indian Military Hospital pause at the statue of the Queen Empress in c. 1914.

THE PRINCE OF WALES UNVEILED THE CHATTRI on 1 February 1921 as a memorial to the Indian soldiers who died at the Royal Pavilion. The Chattri marks the spot where the Hindus and Sikhs were cremated.

A TROOP OF CAVALRY about to fire a salvo to celebrate the coronation of King George V and Queen Mary on 22 June 1911.

STRETCHERS ARE BEING LAID OUT on the platform of Brighton Station in readiness for a convoy of wounded soldiers.

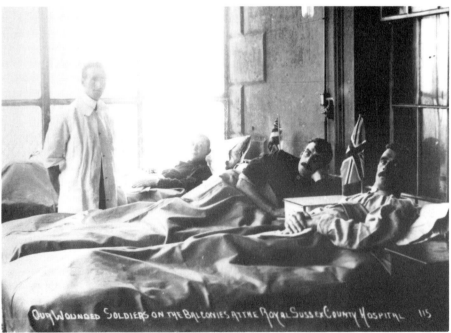

THERE IS NOT A GREAT DEAL OF SPACE BETWEEN THE BEDS occupied by these wounded soldiers at the Royal Sussex Hospital.

THE MONUMENT TO THE MEN OF THE ROYAL SUSSEX REGIMENT who died in the Second Boer War was unveiled in 1904. When Mafeking was relieved in May 1900, Brighton went wild with delight.

THE WAR OFFICE commandeered the playing fields of Windlesham House School, Portslade, in 1914. At one stage the camp played host to 600 mules on their way to the Dardenelles.

THE NEWLY-CREATED BRIGHTON WAR MEMORIAL in the 1920s.

THE SUPREME WAR COUNCIL met at Hove Town Hall on 22 September 1939. Prime Minister Neville Chamberlain is about to step into his car.

HMS King Alfred

THIS PHOTOGRAPH WAS TAKEN IN AUGUST 1938 and shows the building of Hove Marina. It was not until the Admiralty took over the swimming baths in 1939 that the place became HMS *King Alfred*. After the war it seemed pointless to revert to the name 'Hove Marina' when everyone had got used to the new name, so the Admiralty gave permission and the *King Alfred* it has been ever since.

A TEARFUL EXPERIENCE — the result of CPO Vass's lesson on 'gas-masks, use of'.

LEARNING HOW TO USE A SEXTANT on the terrace of the *King Alfred*.

A BREAK FOR SANDWICHES during a lesson in pilotage in the summer of 1940.

CADET RATINGS and the whalers used for training at Portslade in 1940.

THIS GROUP started their training at the *King Alfred* in June 1940. CPO Vass is in the centre. The tall man in the back row is A.T. Lennox-Boyd MP, later a Government minister, and in the second row, second from the right, is Pen Tennyson, a talented film director who was killed in 1941.

CADET RATING IAN HENNELL on guard duty at HMS *King Alfred* in the summer of 1940.

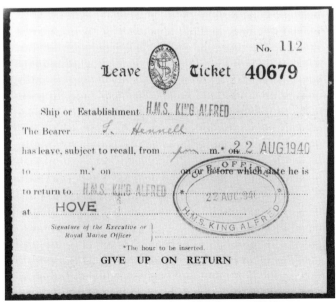

A RARE SCRAP OF MEMORABILIA — a leave ticket dated 22 August 1940.

LEARNING ABOUT SMALL BOATS. The building in the background is the old RNVR depot.

KING GEORGE VI visited HMS *King Alfred* on 29 May 1941. He is followed by Wren Officer Stonham and Captain J.N. Pelly. CPO Vass stands on the left.

PROOF THAT CPO VASS REALLY DID UNBEND once the cadet ratings had achieved officer status. These officers under training seem to be enjoying a good joke, while the photographer for some reason has chosen to lie on the grass and point his camera upwards.

PAY PARADE for the permanent staff of the *King Alfred* took place in the Drill Shed.

DIVISIONS ON A MISTY MORNING at Hove in 1944. On the extreme right is Lieutenant-Commander R. Davey, Field Training Officer.

A NAVIGATION LESSON in progress at the *King Alfred*.

KING ALFRED WRENS on Hove sea front in 1945. From left to right they are Joan Morris, Marjorie Lane, Sylvia Smith, Pat Smeath, Betty Bates and Daisy Ennis.

VICTORY PARADE through Hove in 1945. Leading the column are PO Joyce Tuck on the left and PO Barbara Ford on the right.

ADMIRAL SIR ANDREW BROWNE CUNNINGHAM (known affectionately as ABC) was made an Honorary Freeman of Hove on 5 September 1945.

PAYING-OFF PARTY outside the *King Alfred* in 1945. In the front row: CPO Jones stands second from the left, A.W. Saunders, Administrative Officer, is third from the left and FTO Ray Davey is fourth from the right.

REMOVING THE SHIP'S BELL in 1946.

THE FORMAL OPENING OF THE KING ALFRED SWIMMING BATHS in August 1946. Turning the key of the door is Admiral Sir G. Layton, while the smiling Mayor of Hove (H.C. Andrews) looks on.

SECTION SEVENTEEN

The Rural Scene

LOOKING NORTHWARDS up what later became Holmes Avenue towards West Blatchington windmill c. 1900.

A PEACEFUL SCENE by the pond at Falmer.

BLACK OXEN were once a common sight in Sussex.

THIS PUMP supplied the village drinking-water.

Falmer,   Sussex

FLINT COTTAGES AT FALMER. Flint was one of the traditional building materials in Sussex.

Rottingdean,   Sussex.

THE PHOTOGRAPHER WHO TOOK THIS SHOT was an expert at arranging his models. This study of
Rottingdean has everything.

Cych Gate & Kipling's House,   Rottingdean

THERE ARE SEVERAL POINTS OF INTEREST IN THIS VIEW OF ROTTINGDEAN. There is the windmill on Beacon Hill and below it the house where Sir Edward Burne-Jones lived; then the lychgate and Rudyard Kipling's house on the right.

Patcham.   Sussex.

THE BLACK LION was still advertising good stabling when this photograph was taken. In 1928, Patcham, as well as Falmer and Rottingdean, came within Brighton's boundaries.

FLINT COTTAGES AT PATCHAM. The sign outside the door advertises 'Shelvey's Minerals, sweets and tea'.